NAME:_____

COURSE:_____

STUDENT ID:_____

MY GOAL IS TO GRADUATE _____

_____

_____

CROWN
JOURNALS

Class Schedule

SEMESTER:			YEAR:			
TIME	**MON**	**TUE**	**WED**	**THUS**	**FRI**	**SAT**

NOTES

Class Schedule

SEMESTER:			YEAR:			
TIME	**MON**	**TUE**	**WED**	**THUS**	**FRI**	**SAT**

NOTES

Class Schedule

SEMESTER:			YEAR:			
TIME	**MON**	**TUE**	**WED**	**THUS**	**FRI**	**SAT**

NOTES

Personal Time-Table

SEMESTER:			YEAR:			
TIME	**MON**	**TUE**	**WED**	**THUS**	**FRI**	**SAT**

NOTES

Personal Time-Table

SEMESTER:			YEAR:			
TIME	**MON**	**TUE**	**WED**	**THUS**	**FRI**	**SAT**

NOTES

Personal Time-Table

SEMESTER:		YEAR:				
TIME	**MON**	**TUE**	**WED**	**THUS**	**FRI**	**SAT**

NOTES

Deadlines

DATE DUE	CLASS	TITLE	NOTES

NOTES

Deadlines

DATE DUE	CLASS	TITLE	NOTES

NOTES

Deadlines

DATE DUE	CLASS	TITLE	NOTES

NOTES

Deadlines

DATE DUE	CLASS	TITLE	NOTES

NOTES

Deadlines

DATE DUE	CLASS	TITLE	NOTES

NOTES

Deadlines

DATE DUE	CLASS	TITLE	NOTES

NOTES

Grade Tracker

COURSE	1ST C.A	2ND C.A	3RD C.A	4TH C.A	5TH C.A	EXAM/ PROJECT	TOTAL

C.A: CONTINUOUS ASSESSMENT (INCLUDES TESTS, PRACTICALS, TERM PAPERS, FIELD WORK ETC.)

Grade Tracker

COURSE	1ST C.A	2ND C.A	3RD C.A	4TH C.A	5TH C.A	EXAM/ PROJECT	TOTAL

C.A: CONTINUOUS ASSESSMENT (INCLUDES TESTS, PRACTICALS, TERM PAPERS, FIELD WORK ETC.)

Grade Tracker

COURSE	1ST C.A	2ND C.A	3RD C.A	4TH C.A	5TH C.A	EXAM/ PROJECT	TOTAL

C.A: CONTINUOUS ASSESSMENT (INCLUDES TESTS, PRACTICALS, TERM PAPERS, FIELD WORK ETC.)

Monthly Planner

DAY OF THE WEEK	1ST WEEK	2ND WEEK	3RD WEEK	4TH WEEK	5TH WEEK
MONDAY					
TUESDAY					
WEDNESDAY					
THURSDAY					
FRIDAY					
SATURDAY					
SUNDAY					

Monthly Planner

DAY OF THE WEEK	1ST WEEK	2ND WEEK	3RD WEEK	4TH WEEK	5TH WEEK
MONDAY					
TUESDAY					
WEDNESDAY					
THURSDAY					
FRIDAY					
SATURDAY					
SUNDAY					

Monthly Planner

DAY OF THE WEEK	1ST WEEK	2ND WEEK	3RD WEEK	4TH WEEK	5TH WEEK
MONDAY					
TUESDAY					
WEDNESDAY					
THURSDAY					
FRIDAY					
SATURDAY					
SUNDAY					

Monthly Planner

DAY OF THE WEEK	1ST WEEK	2ND WEEK	3RD WEEK	4TH WEEK	5TH WEEK
MONDAY					
TUESDAY					
WEDNESDAY					
THURSDAY					
FRIDAY					
SATURDAY					
SUNDAY					

Monthly Planner

DAY OF THE WEEK	1ST WEEK	2ND WEEK	3RD WEEK	4TH WEEK	5TH WEEK
MONDAY					
TUESDAY					
WEDNESDAY					
THURSDAY					
FRIDAY					
SATURDAY					
SUNDAY					

Monthly Planner

DAY OF THE WEEK	1ST WEEK	2ND WEEK	3RD WEEK	4TH WEEK	5TH WEEK
MONDAY					
TUESDAY					
WEDNESDAY					
THURSDAY					
FRIDAY					
SATURDAY					
SUNDAY					

Monthly Planner

DAY OF THE WEEK	1ST WEEK	2ND WEEK	3RD WEEK	4TH WEEK	5TH WEEK
MONDAY					
TUESDAY					
WEDNESDAY					
THURSDAY					
FRIDAY					
SATURDAY					
SUNDAY					

Monthly Planner

DAY OF THE WEEK	1ST WEEK	2ND WEEK	3RD WEEK	4TH WEEK	5TH WEEK
MONDAY					
TUESDAY					
WEDNESDAY					
THURSDAY					
FRIDAY					
SATURDAY					
SUNDAY					

Monthly Planner

DAY OF THE WEEK	1ST WEEK	2ND WEEK	3RD WEEK	4TH WEEK	5TH WEEK
MONDAY					
TUESDAY					
WEDNESDAY					
THURSDAY					
FRIDAY					
SATURDAY					
SUNDAY					

Monthly Planner

DAY OF THE WEEK	1ST WEEK	2ND WEEK	3RD WEEK	4TH WEEK	5TH WEEK
MONDAY					
TUESDAY					
WEDNESDAY					
THURSDAY					
FRIDAY					
SATURDAY					
SUNDAY					

Monthly Planner

DAY OF THE WEEK	1ST WEEK	2ND WEEK	3RD WEEK	4TH WEEK	5TH WEEK
MONDAY					
TUESDAY					
WEDNESDAY					
THURSDAY					
FRIDAY					
SATURDAY					
SUNDAY					

Monthly Planner

DAY OF THE WEEK	1ST WEEK	2ND WEEK	3RD WEEK	4TH WEEK	5TH WEEK
MONDAY					
TUESDAY					
WEDNESDAY					
THURSDAY					
FRIDAY					
SATURDAY					
SUNDAY					

Revision/Study Chart

COURSE REFERENCE		LECTURER	
COURSE TITLE			
COURSE OBJECTIVE		EXAM	
LEVEL		SEMESTER	

Date Due	Topic	Completed

Revision/Study Chart

COURSE REFERENCE		LECTURER	
COURSE TITLE			
COURSE OBJECTIVE		EXAM	
LEVEL		SEMESTER	

Date Due	Topic	Completed

Revision/Study Chart

COURSE REFERENCE		LECTURER	
COURSE TITLE			
COURSE OBJECTIVE		EXAM	
LEVEL		SEMESTER	

Date Due	Topic	Completed

Revision Group

Name	Phone Number	Course

NOTES

Revision Group

Name	Phone Number	Course

NOTES

Revision Group

Name	Phone Number	Course

NOTES

Revision Group

Name	Phone Number	Course

NOTES

Revision Group

Name	Phone Number	Course

NOTES

Revision Group

Name	Phone Number	Course

NOTES

Course Grade Goals

SESSION		SEMESTER	
LEVEL		EXAM DATE	

#	Course Code & Title	Grades

Course Grade Goals

SESSION		SEMESTER	
LEVEL		EXAM DATE	

#	Course Code & Title	Grades

Course Grade Goals

SESSION		SEMESTER	
LEVEL		EXAM DATE	

#	Course Code & Title	Grades

Class Schedule

SEMESTER:				YEAR:			

TIME	MON	TUE	WED	THUS	FRI	SAT

NOTES

Class Schedule

SEMESTER:	YEAR:

TIME	MON	TUE	WED	THUS	FRI	SAT

NOTES

Class Schedule

TIME	MON	TUE	WED	THUS	FRI	SAT

NOTES

Personal Time-Table

SEMESTER:			YEAR:			
TIME	**MON**	**TUE**	**WED**	**THUS**	**FRI**	**SAT**

NOTES

Personal Time-Table

SEMESTER:

YEAR:

TIME	MON	TUE	WED	THUS	FRI	SAT

NOTES

Personal Time-Table

SEMESTER:		YEAR:				
TIME	**MON**	**TUE**	**WED**	**THUS**	**FRI**	**SAT**

NOTES

Deadlines

DATE DUE	CLASS	TITLE	NOTES

NOTES

Deadlines

DATE DUE	CLASS	TITLE	NOTES

NOTES

Deadlines

DATE DUE	CLASS	TITLE	NOTES

NOTES

Deadlines

DATE DUE	CLASS	TITLE	NOTES

NOTES

Deadlines

DATE DUE	CLASS	TITLE	NOTES

NOTES

Deadlines

DATE DUE	CLASS	TITLE	NOTES

NOTES

Grade Tracker

COURSE	1ST C.A	2ND C.A	3RD C.A	4TH C.A	5TH C.A	EXAM/ PROJECT	TOTAL

C.A: CONTINUOUS ASSESSMENT (INCLUDES TESTS, PRACTICALS, TERM PAPERS, FIELD WORK ETC.)

Grade Tracker

COURSE	1ST C.A	2ND C.A	3RD C.A	4TH C.A	5TH C.A	EXAM/ PROJECT	TOTAL

C.A: CONTINUOUS ASSESSMENT (INCLUDES TESTS, PRACTICALS, TERM PAPERS, FIELD WORK ETC.)

Grade Tracker

COURSE	1ST C.A	2ND C.A	3RD C.A	4TH C.A	5TH C.A	EXAM/ PROJECT	TOTAL

C.A: CONTINUOUS ASSESSMENT (INCLUDES TESTS, PRACTICALS, TERM PAPERS, FIELD WORK ETC.)

Monthly Planner

DAY OF THE WEEK	1ST WEEK	2ND WEEK	3RD WEEK	4TH WEEK	5TH WEEK
MONDAY					
TUESDAY					
WEDNESDAY					
THURSDAY					
FRIDAY					
SATURDAY					
SUNDAY					

Monthly Planner

DAY OF THE WEEK	1ST WEEK	2ND WEEK	3RD WEEK	4TH WEEK	5TH WEEK
MONDAY					
TUESDAY					
WEDNESDAY					
THURSDAY					
FRIDAY					
SATURDAY					
SUNDAY					

Monthly Planner

DAY OF THE WEEK	1ST WEEK	2ND WEEK	3RD WEEK	4TH WEEK	5TH WEEK
MONDAY					
TUESDAY					
WEDNESDAY					
THURSDAY					
FRIDAY					
SATURDAY					
SUNDAY					

Monthly Planner

DAY OF THE WEEK	1ST WEEK	2ND WEEK	3RD WEEK	4TH WEEK	5TH WEEK
MONDAY					
TUESDAY					
WEDNESDAY					
THURSDAY					
FRIDAY					
SATURDAY					
SUNDAY					

Monthly Planner

DAY OF THE WEEK	1ST WEEK	2ND WEEK	3RD WEEK	4TH WEEK	5TH WEEK
MONDAY					
TUESDAY					
WEDNESDAY					
THURSDAY					
FRIDAY					
SATURDAY					
SUNDAY					

Monthly Planner

DAY OF THE WEEK	1ST WEEK	2ND WEEK	3RD WEEK	4TH WEEK	5TH WEEK
MONDAY					
TUESDAY					
WEDNESDAY					
THURSDAY					
FRIDAY					
SATURDAY					
SUNDAY					

Monthly Planner

DAY OF THE WEEK	1ST WEEK	2ND WEEK	3RD WEEK	4TH WEEK	5TH WEEK
MONDAY					
TUESDAY					
WEDNESDAY					
THURSDAY					
FRIDAY					
SATURDAY					
SUNDAY					

Monthly Planner

DAY OF THE WEEK	1ST WEEK	2ND WEEK	3RD WEEK	4TH WEEK	5TH WEEK
MONDAY					
TUESDAY					
WEDNESDAY					
THURSDAY					
FRIDAY					
SATURDAY					
SUNDAY					

Monthly Planner

DAY OF THE WEEK	1ST WEEK	2ND WEEK	3RD WEEK	4TH WEEK	5TH WEEK
MONDAY					
TUESDAY					
WEDNESDAY					
THURSDAY					
FRIDAY					
SATURDAY					
SUNDAY					

Monthly Planner

DAY OF THE WEEK	1ST WEEK	2ND WEEK	3RD WEEK	4TH WEEK	5TH WEEK
MONDAY					
TUESDAY					
WEDNESDAY					
THURSDAY					
FRIDAY					
SATURDAY					
SUNDAY					

Monthly Planner

DAY OF THE WEEK	1ST WEEK	2ND WEEK	3RD WEEK	4TH WEEK	5TH WEEK
MONDAY					
TUESDAY					
WEDNESDAY					
THURSDAY					
FRIDAY					
SATURDAY					
SUNDAY					

Monthly Planner

DAY OF THE WEEK	1ST WEEK	2ND WEEK	3RD WEEK	4TH WEEK	5TH WEEK
MONDAY					
TUESDAY					
WEDNESDAY					
THURSDAY					
FRIDAY					
SATURDAY					
SUNDAY					

Revision/Study Chart

COURSE REFERENCE		LECTURER	
COURSE TITLE			
COURSE OBJECTIVE		EXAM	
LEVEL		SEMESTER	

Date Due	Topic	Completed

Revision/Study Chart

COURSE REFERENCE		LECTURER	
COURSE TITLE			
COURSE OBJECTIVE		EXAM	
LEVEL		SEMESTER	

Date Due	Topic	Completed

Revision/Study Chart

COURSE REFERENCE		LECTURER	
COURSE TITLE			
COURSE OBJECTIVE		EXAM	
LEVEL		SEMESTER	

Date Due	Topic	Completed

Revision Group

Name	Phone Number	Course

NOTES

Revision Group

Name	Phone Number	Course

NOTES

Revision Group

Name	Phone Number	Course

NOTES

Revision Group

Name	Phone Number	Course

NOTES

Revision Group

Name	Phone Number	Course

NOTES

Revision Group

Name	Phone Number	Course

NOTES

Course Grade Goals

SESSION		SEMESTER	
LEVEL		EXAM DATE	

#	Course Code & Title	Grades

Course Grade Goals

SESSION		SEMESTER	
LEVEL		EXAM DATE	

#	Course Code & Title	Grades

Course Grade Goals

SESSION		SEMESTER	
LEVEL		EXAM DATE	

#	Course Code & Title	Grades

Class Schedule

SEMESTER:		YEAR:				
TIME	**MON**	**TUE**	**WED**	**THUS**	**FRI**	**SAT**

NOTES

Class Schedule

SEMESTER:			YEAR:			
TIME	**MON**	**TUE**	**WED**	**THUS**	**FRI**	**SAT**

NOTES

Class Schedule

| SEMESTER: | | | YEAR: | | | |

TIME	MON	TUE	WED	THUS	FRI	SAT

NOTES

Personal Time-Table

SEMESTER:		YEAR:				
TIME	MON	TUE	WED	THUS	FRI	SAT

NOTES

Personal Time-Table

SEMESTER:			YEAR:			
TIME	MON	TUE	WED	THUS	FRI	SAT

NOTES

Personal Time-Table

SEMESTER:			YEAR:			

TIME	MON	TUE	WED	THUS	FRI	SAT

NOTES

Deadlines

DATE DUE	CLASS	TITLE	NOTES

NOTES

Deadlines

DATE DUE	CLASS	TITLE	NOTES

NOTES

Deadlines

DATE DUE	CLASS	TITLE	NOTES

NOTES

Deadlines

DATE DUE	CLASS	TITLE	NOTES

NOTES

Deadlines

DATE DUE	CLASS	TITLE	NOTES

NOTES

Deadlines

DATE DUE	CLASS	TITLE	NOTES

NOTES

Grade Tracker

COURSE	1ST C.A	2ND C.A	3RD C.A	4TH C.A	5TH C.A	EXAM/ PROJECT	TOTAL

C.A: CONTINUOUS ASSESSMENT (INCLUDES TESTS, PRACTICALS, TERM PAPERS, FIELD WORK ETC.)

Grade Tracker

COURSE	1ST C.A	2ND C.A	3RD C.A	4TH C.A	5TH C.A	EXAM/ PROJECT	TOTAL

C.A: CONTINUOUS ASSESSMENT (INCLUDES TESTS, PRACTICALS, TERM PAPERS, FIELD WORK ETC.)

Grade Tracker

COURSE	1ST C.A	2ND C.A	3RD C.A	4TH C.A	5TH C.A	EXAM/ PROJECT	TOTAL

C.A: CONTINUOUS ASSESSMENT (INCLUDES TESTS, PRACTICALS, TERM PAPERS, FIELD WORK ETC.)

Monthly Planner

DAY OF THE WEEK	1ST WEEK	2ND WEEK	3RD WEEK	4TH WEEK	5TH WEEK
MONDAY					
TUESDAY					
WEDNESDAY					
THURSDAY					
FRIDAY					
SATURDAY					
SUNDAY					

Monthly Planner

DAY OF THE WEEK	1ST WEEK	2ND WEEK	3RD WEEK	4TH WEEK	5TH WEEK
MONDAY					
TUESDAY					
WEDNESDAY					
THURSDAY					
FRIDAY					
SATURDAY					
SUNDAY					

Monthly Planner

DAY OF THE WEEK	1ST WEEK	2ND WEEK	3RD WEEK	4TH WEEK	5TH WEEK
MONDAY					
TUESDAY					
WEDNESDAY					
THURSDAY					
FRIDAY					
SATURDAY					
SUNDAY					

Monthly Planner

DAY OF THE WEEK	1ST WEEK	2ND WEEK	3RD WEEK	4TH WEEK	5TH WEEK
MONDAY					
TUESDAY					
WEDNESDAY					
THURSDAY					
FRIDAY					
SATURDAY					
SUNDAY					

Monthly Planner

DAY OF THE WEEK	1ST WEEK	2ND WEEK	3RD WEEK	4TH WEEK	5TH WEEK
MONDAY					
TUESDAY					
WEDNESDAY					
THURSDAY					
FRIDAY					
SATURDAY					
SUNDAY					

Monthly Planner

DAY OF THE WEEK	1ST WEEK	2ND WEEK	3RD WEEK	4TH WEEK	5TH WEEK
MONDAY					
TUESDAY					
WEDNESDAY					
THURSDAY					
FRIDAY					
SATURDAY					
SUNDAY					

Monthly Planner

DAY OF THE WEEK	1ST WEEK	2ND WEEK	3RD WEEK	4TH WEEK	5TH WEEK
MONDAY					
TUESDAY					
WEDNESDAY					
THURSDAY					
FRIDAY					
SATURDAY					
SUNDAY					

Monthly Planner

DAY OF THE WEEK	1ST WEEK	2ND WEEK	3RD WEEK	4TH WEEK	5TH WEEK
MONDAY					
TUESDAY					
WEDNESDAY					
THURSDAY					
FRIDAY					
SATURDAY					
SUNDAY					

Monthly Planner

DAY OF THE WEEK	1ST WEEK	2ND WEEK	3RD WEEK	4TH WEEK	5TH WEEK
MONDAY					
TUESDAY					
WEDNESDAY					
THURSDAY					
FRIDAY					
SATURDAY					
SUNDAY					

Monthly Planner

DAY OF THE WEEK	1ST WEEK	2ND WEEK	3RD WEEK	4TH WEEK	5TH WEEK
MONDAY					
TUESDAY					
WEDNESDAY					
THURSDAY					
FRIDAY					
SATURDAY					
SUNDAY					

Monthly Planner

ELEVENTH MONTH

DAY OF THE WEEK	1ST WEEK	2ND WEEK	3RD WEEK	4TH WEEK	5TH WEEK
MONDAY					
TUESDAY					
WEDNESDAY					
THURSDAY					
FRIDAY					
SATURDAY					
SUNDAY					

Monthly Planner

DAY OF THE WEEK	1ST WEEK	2ND WEEK	3RD WEEK	4TH WEEK	5TH WEEK
MONDAY					
TUESDAY					
WEDNESDAY					
THURSDAY					
FRIDAY					
SATURDAY					
SUNDAY					

Revision/Study Chart

COURSE REFERENCE		LECTURER	
COURSE TITLE			
COURSE OBJECTIVE		EXAM	
LEVEL		SEMESTER	

Date Due	Topic	Completed

Revision/Study Chart

COURSE REFERENCE		LECTURER	
COURSE TITLE			
COURSE OBJECTIVE		EXAM	
LEVEL		SEMESTER	

Date Due	Topic	Completed

Revision/Study Chart

COURSE REFERENCE		LECTURER	
COURSE TITLE			
COURSE OBJECTIVE		EXAM	
LEVEL		SEMESTER	

Date Due	Topic	Completed

Revision Group

Name	Phone Number	Course

NOTES

Revision Group

Name	Phone Number	Course

NOTES

Revision Group

Name	Phone Number	Course

NOTES

Revision Group

Name	Phone Number	Course

NOTES

Revision Group

Name	Phone Number	Course

NOTES

Revision Group

Name	Phone Number	Course

NOTES

Course Grade Goals

SESSION		SEMESTER	
LEVEL		EXAM DATE	

#	Course Code & Title	Grades

Course Grade Goals

SESSION		SEMESTER	
LEVEL		EXAM DATE	

#	Course Code & Title	Grades

Course Grade Goals

SESSION		SEMESTER	
LEVEL		EXAM DATE	

#	Course Code & Title	Grades

Notes

Notes

Printed in Great Britain
by Amazon

83784360R00072